Asian American WOMEN OF ACHIEVEMENT

Sara Rowe Mount

San Diego, CA

© 2026 ReferencePoint Press, Inc.
Printed in the United States

For more information, contact:
ReferencePoint Press, Inc.
PO Box 27779
San Diego, CA 92198
www.ReferencePointPress.com

ALL RIGHTS RESERVED.
No part of this work covered by the copyright hereon may be reproduced or used in any form or by any means—graphic, electronic, or mechanical, including photocopying, recording, taping, web distribution, or information storage retrieval systems—without the written permission of the publisher.

LIBRARY OF CONGRESS CATALOGING-IN-PUBLICATION DATA

Names: Mount, Sara Rowe author
Title: Asian American women of achievement / by Sara Rowe Mount.
Description: San Diego, CA : ReferencePoint Press, Inc, 2026. | Series: Part of the Women of Achievement series | Includes bibliographical references and index.
Identifiers: LCCN 2025005304 (print) | LCCN 2025005305 (ebook) | ISBN 9781678210540 lib. bdg. | ISBN 9781678210557 ebook
Subjects: LCSH: Asian Americans--Juvenile literature | Mink, Patsy T., 1927-2002--Biography--Juvenile literature | Wong-Staal, Flossie--Biography--Juvenile literature | Han, Jenny--Biography--Juvenile literature | Sui, Anna--Biography--Juvenile literature | Kaling, Mindy--Biography--Juvenile literature | LCGFT: Biographies
Classification: LCC E184.O6 M68 2026 (print) | LCC E184.O6 (ebook) | DDC 305.48/89510922--dc23/eng/20250321
LC record available at https://lccn.loc.gov/2025005304
LC ebook record available at https://lccn.loc.gov/2025005305

CONTENTS

Leading the Way

Asian American women have not only had to overcome discrimination for their gender but have also experienced racism and prejudice stemming from their ethnic and cultural background. These women represent a diverse and culturally rich segment of the US population, and their contributions to our society reflect the same. Their accomplishments span impactful discoveries in the fields of medicine and science, advocacy for the rights of women and minorities, and contributions to the arts.

Out of This World

As a girl growing up in the 1960s and 1970s, Kalpana Chawla had big dreams of flying and exploring the night sky, ones that would one day take her to outer space. "For me, it was very far-fetched to think I get to fly on the space shuttle because I lived in India in a very small town," Chawla once said, reflecting on her childhood. "And forget about space. I didn't even know if my folks were going to let me go to the engineering college."[1] While her parents wanted her to pursue higher education, her father believed that engineering was a man's field. But go to college she did, receiving a bachelor of science degree in aeronautical engineering from Punjab Engineering College in 1982. Her further education took her to the United States, where she earned a master's degree and a doctorate in aeronautical engineering from the University of Texas and University of Colorado, respectively, in 1984 and 1988. After working as an aeronautical engineer for several years, in 1994 Chawla was one of twenty applicants chosen out of four thousand for a coveted spot in the National Aeronautics and Space Administration's astronaut program.

> "For me, it was very far-fetched to think I get to fly on the space shuttle because I lived in India in a very small town. And forget about space. I didn't even know if my folks were going to let me go to the engineering college."[1]
>
> —Kalpana Chawla, astronaut

In November 1997 Chawla became the first Indian American woman to travel to space when she flew on mission STS-87. In January 2003 she returned to space and helped conduct experiments on the effects of low gravity. Over the course of these two flights, Chawla was in space for 30 days, 14 hours, and 54 minutes. Tragically, on February 1, 2003, Chawla and the rest of the *Columbia* crew lost their lives when the shuttle broke apart upon reentry to the earth's atmosphere. Over twenty years later, her passion, drive, and accomplishments still inspire girls with an interest in STEM fields, especially those of Indian descent. "One of her favourite sayings was 'reach for the stars,' and it was something she often wrote when she was asked for an autograph," says her sister-in-law Anjali Chawla. "She absolutely loved children, and today, this is exactly what she would tell all the young people who are inspired by her."[2]

Peace Found in Painting

Born in Japan in 1907, Hisako Shimizu Hibi immigrated to the United States with her family when she was thirteen, eventually settling in California. When the rest of her family returned to Japan in 1925, Hibi remained and attended high school, where she learned English and immersed herself in painting as an outlet for self-expression. After graduation, she attended the California School of Fine Arts, where she studied oil painting and met her future husband, George Matsusaburo Hibi.

Upheaval occurred in the family of Hisako, George, and their two children when they were forcibly interned along with many other Japanese Americans in 1942. During their three-year internment, Hibi taught art to hundreds of children, teens, and adults at the Topaz internment camp art school. She also continued to work on her own paintings. Her daughter, Ibuki, later said of her painting style, "She was able to paint in an abstract

Kalpana Chawla was the first Indian American to travel to space. She is shown here on the space shuttle Columbia*'s aft flight deck in 1997.*

style, relying only on the art elements of color, form, and line in order to express her feelings and thoughts. She believed in the power of art to create peace of mind, and she wanted to convey a good feeling to onlookers, who would take the time to study her paintings."[3] Hibi's paintings of the experiences of Japanese Americans in internment camps are now some of the most well known of her paintings and are displayed in museums such as the Smithsonian American Art Museum and the Japanese American National Museum. Hibi's paintings provide a testimony to resilience and fortitude, but also memorialize a time of terrible civil rights violations in American history, reminding us that no one should be judged or discriminated against for their race or ethnic background. Hibi said in an inscription on her painting *Floating Clouds*, "Free, free, I want to be free; free as the clouds I see up above Topaz."[4] She wanted to be free of both the internment camp and this racial discrimination.

Hisako Shimizu Hibi and Kalpana Chawla are just two women of Asian heritage who made tremendous contributions in science and art to the United States. The five other women featured in this book provide further glimpses into the talent, passion, and innovation that Asian American women have brought to their respective fields of politics, science, literature, fashion, and film. Their discoveries and creations have furthered the rights and ambitions of women of all races in the United States and continue to provide inspiration to the girls and women of today.

Patsy Mink, US Representative

Over her lifetime, Patsy Mink was devoted to achieving equality, both between men and women and among those of all races in the United States. In 1960 she was chosen to give the speech on civil rights for the Democratic National Convention in Los Angeles, in which she said, "If to believe in freedom and equality is to be a radical, then I am a radical. . . . We must remain steadfast, till all shades of man may stand side by side in dignity and self-respect to truly enjoy the fruits of this great land."[5] In her time in Congress, she was able propose and pass legislation that did just that.

Growing Up Independent

Patsy Takemoto was born on December 6, 1927, in Paia, Hawaii, to Mitama Tateyama and Suematsu Takemoto. Patsy and her brother, Eugene, were third-generation Japanese Americans. In 1922 her father was the first Japanese American to receive a degree in civil engineering at the University of Hawaii and worked as an engineer on a sugar plantation. Patsy's life in a cottage on the plantation where her father worked was privileged in comparison to many other Japanese Americans in Hawaii who lived in segregated plantation camps, but the strict racial and class lines still impacted her family. Her father was the only Japanese American on the plantation's otherwise White managerial staff and was passed over time and time again for the chief engineer role.

> "If to believe in freedom and equality is to be a radical, then I am a radical. . . . We must remain steadfast, till all shades of man may stand side by side in dignity and self-respect to truly enjoy the fruits of this great land."[5]
>
> —Patsy Mink

Another distinct difference between her upbringing and those of many other Japanese American girls was that while she was expected to learn skills expected of girls at the time, such as sewing and cooking, she was also encouraged to be strong and assertive, rather than ladylike and submissive. Patsy and Eugene were treated as equals by their parents, and her brother often included her in more boyish activities, such as bike riding and baseball and football games with his friends. Recalling her childhood with her parents, Patsy later said, "They encouraged us in all sorts of activities—scouting and piano lessons, hula lessons, ukulele lessons. And, just about everything that we showed interest in, they would seize upon that, and encourage us to go on to try to develop our skills."[6]

Patsy was independent and assertive from a young age. At four she insisted that she was ready to go to school with her big brother, who was a year older. Patsy's parents received special permission from the principal at Hāmākua Poko School for her to attend as well. When Eugene and Patsy were in fourth grade, they began attending Kaunoa English Standard School, which at the time was 95 percent White students and had an all-White staff. Admission was by examination of English fluency, and non-White students were often denied entrance. While Patsy excelled academically, she felt isolated at school and found solace reading and listening to radio programs.

The December 7, 1941, Japanese attack on the military base at Pearl Harbor catapulted the United States into World War II and had a massive impact on the lives of Japanese Americans living in the United States and its territories. Suddenly, individuals like Patsy's engineer father were considered suspicious and potentially dangerous. Soon after the attack on Pearl Harbor, when Patsy was fourteen, her father was brought in for questioning. Although he was allowed to return home the next day, her family feared for

Patsy Mink, shown here in 1994, worked to promote equality in the United States.

their future. Patsy watched her father burn his Japanese mementos, a memory that stayed with her for years to come. Later she reflected, "It made me realize that one could not take citizenship and the promise of the US Constitution for granted."[7]

As a teen, Patsy attended Maui High School, where she still succeeded academically and was also much happier. During her senior year she became her school's first female student body president, and she graduated as valedictorian in 1944. Looking back on this, her first run for office, she reflected, "Like most of the decisions I've made in politics, it seemed like a good idea at that time. Why not? The football team backed me, that's why I won."[8]

"It made me realize that one could not take citizenship and the promise of the US Constitution for granted."[7]

—Patsy Mink

Overcoming Obstacles

Patsy entered college at the University of Hawaii with the desire to eventually become a doctor. During her first two years of college, she performed well in her courses and was elected president of the campus Pre-Medical Students Club.

Many of her fellow students chose to transfer to mainland US schools after the end of the 1945–1946 school year, since World War II had prevented many students from applying to colleges outside of Hawaii. Patsy followed suit, transferring to a small college, Wilson College in Pennsylvania. During her sole semester there, Patsy was miserable. She was unhappy with both the academic environment and the racist assumptions that were made about her, beginning with the college president's original choice to house her in a private room because he assumed she spoke little English.

Dissatisfied at Wilson College, Patsy transferred to the University of Nebraska, where her experience was even more challenging. She discovered that all non-White students were housed in the International House dorm, segregating them from White students. Angered by this realization, Patsy began a letter-writing campaign and spoke out about the discriminatory practice. She also ran and won the role of president of the Unaffiliated Students of the University of Nebraska. She later described herself as "the campus Mata Hari" during that time, "somebody who was going to stir up trouble."[9] The college's board of regents eventually revoked the practice of segregated student housing that year. Ultimately, a diagnosis of a thyroid condition brought Patsy back to Hawaii for surgery. She decided to return to the University of Hawaii and completed her degree in zoology and chemistry in 1948.

Despite excellent grades, Patsy's ambitions to become a doctor were thwarted when she was not accepted to any of the medical schools she applied to. She later remembered it as "the most devastating disappointment in my life."[10] After she had worked for several months as a typist at the Honolulu Academy of Arts, a coworker suggested that she consider applying to law school. Although it was very late to apply for the fall semester, Patsy sent

Eli Lilly Company Lawsuit

In 1976 Mink received the disturbing news that during her pregnancy in 1951 she had been part of a drug trial without her knowledge. She and a thousand women receiving prenatal care at the University of Chicago had been given pills that they were told were vitamins but that actually contained diethylstilbestrol. Years later researchers discovered that this drug was causing cancer in both the women and their children. Mink was angered by this knowledge and used her legal background to bring a class action suit against both the University of Chicago and the drug company, Eli Lilly. The case was settled out of court and resulted in both the women and their children being guaranteed no cost diagnostic testing and treatment of any resulting cancer at the Chicago Lying-In Clinic.

in an application to Columbia University and the University of Chicago. She was accepted to the University of Chicago under a foreign student quota, which was technically inaccurate, but Patsy took the opportunity to be one of two women in her law school class. She did not enjoy the grueling law school experience or harsh Chicago winters, but she persevered. While at the University of Chicago, she met her future husband, John Francis Mink, who was studying for a doctorate in geophysics. Patsy graduated with a law degree and married John in 1951.

Motivated by the bleak job prospects and the birth of her only daughter, Gwendolyn, whom they nicknamed Wendy, in 1952 Patsy and her husband moved back to her home of Hawaii. However, even after she passed the bar exam in Hawaii, she was unable to find a job as a lawyer, which she believed was due to discrimination and her interracial marriage. As a result, she decided instead to start her own law firm and became the first Asian American woman to practice law in the territory of Hawaii.

Becoming Political

Discrimination due to both her gender and race fueled Mink's interest in advocating for marginalized individuals. Lack of business at her law firm meant that she often took on court-appointed cases, including divorce and adoption cases. Mink's emergence into politics was a direct result of her recognition that her professional career was reliant on her fighting for change. "I didn't start off wanting to be in politics. I wanted to be a learned professional, serving the community," she once told a reporter. "But they weren't hiring women just then. Not being able to get a job from anybody changed things."[11]

For years Hawaii's politics had been controlled by the Republican Party, but a shift was occurring and Mink wanted to be involved. She founded the Oahu Young Democrats, eventually becoming chair of the territory-wide Young Democrats and in 1957 the vice president of the National Young Democrats. In 1954 Mink worked almost full time on John A. Burns's campaign to replace Hawaii's Republican delegate to the US Congress. Although he was defeated, the experience propelled her into more involvement in Hawaii's politics.

Her work as a staff attorney for the territorial legislature and her disappointment in the performance of several of the legislators led to her first run for office in 1956. At that time, the territorial legislature was all male and almost all White, which made her candidacy as a Japanese American woman an uphill battle. Mink remembered of that run, "I faced overwhelming odds: I was not from a political family, and I had no visible support in the community, no organizational support."[12] Realizing that gaining the support of individual constituents was critical to her success, Mink began a door-to-door campaign, talking to voters and gathering enough support to win a seat in the territorial House of Representatives. In 1958 and 1962 she also ran successfully for a seat in the territorial Senate.

A new opportunity to become involved in national politics arose in 1959 when Hawaii became a state and had two Senate seats and one House seat to fill. She did not win her first run for the House of Representatives that year, although she won the primary and general elections in her next run for a US House seat in 1964, despite once again not being the favored candidate. Mink was the first woman of color elected to Congress and ended up serving for twelve terms in Congress, six in the House and six in the Senate.

Mink's Impact in Congress

Mink's time in Washington was characterized by building relationships and alliances in and out of Congress. She prioritized listening to the needs of her constituents by making frequent trips back to Hawaii and was passionate about advocating for the causes of the marginalized. "She had a passion for her causes and her work, and she never gave up," says Dan Boylan, a Hawaii historian and author. "I was always struck by her sense of, 'Well, we lost today but we're going to win the next time.'. . . She was a principled politician."[13] Her time in Congress began with her aligning herself with the other women in Congress. One cause they took on was a basic one, the right to be able to utilize the congressional gym as men staff members did, without restrictions. Mink says of that victory, "It was just a symbolic gesture that there are so many ways in which sex discrimination manifests itself in the form of social custom, mores or whatever, that you really have to make an issue whenever it strikes you to protest it."[14]

Mink's legacy is considered to be the bills she sponsored and authored that helped women gain more rights in the United

This 1960 photo shows Mink with other women in Congress. She was the first woman of color elected to Congress.

The Impact of Title IX

Title IX's ban on gender-based discrimination has had a large impact on the educational experience of girls and women since its passing, including the following:

- Schools increasing opportunities for women's sports teams, providing more equal funding and support, including scholarships for female athletes
- Removing gender barriers to admittance for colleges and college programs
- Requiring federally funded colleges to investigate charges of sexual harassment and assault
- Expanding protections to also prevent discrimination related to sexual orientation or gender identity

Historian Susan Ware notes that Title IX advocates for the elimination of discrimination and abuse. She says, "Title IX has had a transformative impact on many aspects of women's experience in higher education, starting with sports but then later engaging with issues of sexual harassment and sexual violence on campus. It really has made a very large difference."

Quoted in Alvin Powell, "How Title IX Transformed Colleges, Universities over Past 50 Years," *Harvard Gazette*, June 22, 2022. https://news.harvard.edu.

States. She believed that women's rights were just another segment of civil rights. Today she is remembered for her contributions authoring Title IX, which was passed by Congress in 1972, and its follow-up bill, the Women's Educational Equity Act, in 1974. This landmark piece of legislation said, "No person in the United States shall, on the basis of sex, be excluded from participation in, be denied the benefits of, or be subjected to discrimination under any education program or activity receiving Federal financial assistance."[15]

While she certainly prioritized collaboration with like-minded colleagues, Mink was an outspoken woman of conviction who championed underrepresented voices. She was vocal about these convictions, even if they were not in line with the priorities or views of the Democratic Party. During her terms in Congress,

Mink was most passionate about introducing legislation for causes such as education, childcare, the environment, and programs that supported low-income individuals. These were issues that were especially important to her as a mother, a woman, a Japanese American, and a Hawaiian. Her desire for peace for the United States and its people meant Mink was one of the small minority in Congress who opposed the Vietnam War. She both attempted to

Mink often championed underrepresented voices. This 1995 photo of her was taken at a Capitol Hill rally to protest proposed welfare legislation.

block funding for the war and cosponsored an unsuccessful bill to withdraw military forces from Vietnam, which displeased many of her constituents.

After serving in the House of Representatives for twelve years, Mink lost a race for a seat in the Senate and served in other roles in the national government. Eventually, she won the Senate seat left vacant by the death of Senator Spark Matsunaga in 1990. To the end of her terms, she continued to advocate for the civil rights of all US citizens. She was a vocal opponent to the governmental response to the terrorist attacks on 9/11, including the creation of the US Department of Homeland Security, because she believed they presented a risk to civil liberties.

"She was the great voice and advocate of women's rights, not just freedom of choice but college sports. She was a great voice for peace and education, and she will be sorely missed in the Congress."[16]

—Dan Inouye, US senator from Hawaii

Mink served for twelve years in the Senate, until her death from pneumonia on September 28, 2002. Due to the timing of her death, she was still on the ballot for the November election. The beloved former congresswoman won by a landslide and had to be replaced by special election the following year. Fellow Hawaiian senator Dan Inouye said of her passing, "It's a great loss for Hawai'i and our nation. . . . She was the great voice and advocate of women's rights, not just freedom of choice but college sports. She was a great voice for peace and education, and she will be sorely missed in the Congress."[16]

Flossie Wong-Staal, Scientist

As a young girl in China, Yee Ching Wong had a wide range of interests, from literature and poetry to science. But the high school system in Hong Kong required students to choose between a science or nonscience track. "So, part of the mentality is that if you're smart, you should go into science. . . . And people . . . usually accept that because they feel it's an honor and a privilege," she reflected years later. "So I can say that it's almost by default that I was . . . in the science path. . . . But I, of course, never regretted it."[17] This teenager would grow up to be a groundbreaking scientist who would save lives with her discoveries.

An Interest in Science Grows

On August 27, 1946, Yee Ching Wong was born in Guangzhou, the third-largest city in China, to father Sueh-Fung Wong and mother Wei-Chung Chor. She was the third of four children. Her father worked in the export-import business, and her mother was a homemaker. Her family's life was disrupted, as many others were, by the 1949 Chinese Communist Revolution, and in 1952 her family moved away from mainland China to Hong Kong to escape restrictions put in place by the Communist Party.

When Yee Ching graduated from Maryknoll Sisters School, where she had excelled in the science program, her high school teachers encouraged her to pursue higher education outside of China. Encouraged to Westernize her first name, she chose to call herself Flossie. Flossie immersed herself in her studies at the University of California, Los Angeles (UCLA), which she chose because friends were also attending and because of her familiarity with California from the American movies and TV she had watched. Initially, she struggled with both the cultural differences and the language, but she focused on her study of microbiology and bacteriology and completed her coursework in three years, graduating with honors with a bachelor's degree in bacteriology in 1968. She was the first woman in her family to obtain a college degree, and she would continue to break boundaries during her career. Flossie immediately began to study for her PhD in molecular biology. It was an exciting time of new discovery in the field and for Flossie, as she later remembered: "I think there was cloning discovered with the restriction enzymes, so things are just becoming possible . . . the ability to purify genes and to amplify

Flossie Wong-Staal took the science path in high school and became a groundbreaking scientist.

them enough to study every detail was something that wasn't possible before. . . . [It was] revolutionary and open[ed] up all kinds of possibilities."[18] After she received her PhD in 1972, she completed postdoctoral research at the University of California, San Diego (UCSD).

A Time of New Discoveries

In 1971 Wong-Staal had married her first husband, Stephen P. Staal, whom she had met at UCLA while studying for her PhD. His assignment to the National Institutes of Health (NIH) and their move to Bethesda, Maryland, in 1973 ended up impacting the trajectory of Wong-Staal's career. She applied for and obtained a Fogarty Fellowship at Robert Gallo's National Cancer Institute, which was also part of the NIH. Wong-Staal and Gallo worked well together, and their partnership was prolific. They coauthored over one hundred journal articles featuring their studies over the next twenty years. *The Scientist* magazine later determined in 1990 that she was the female scientist who had been the most cited by other researchers over the 1980s, with 7,772 citations. "She came as a postdoc, and she was the best I ever saw—before, during, or after," Gallo said of Wong-Staal. "She was really sharp in things I needed to be sharper in. [Due to her contributions] we became among the most productive labs in the 20th century."[19]

> **"The ability to purify genes and to amplify them enough to study every detail was something that wasn't possible before. . . . [It was] revolutionary and open[ed] up all kinds of possibilities."[18]**
>
> **—Flossie Wong-Staal**

During the years Wong-Staal spent in postgraduate study and working at the NIH, she also took on the challenge of motherhood. Her daughter Stephanie was born in 1972 and Caroline in 1983. The 1970s and 1980s were also a time of prolific research and new discoveries for Wong-Staal. Wong-Staal's early study at the NIH focused on primate retroviruses such as the gibbon ape leukemia virus, in the hope that the knowledge gained could be applied to humans. A key finding during this research was the

Flossie Westernizes Her Name

The suggestion for Yee Ching Wong to Westernize her name is not an unusual one. In fact, many immigrants, especially those of Asian descent, are encouraged to choose easier-to-pronounce "American" names as alternatives to their given ones. Some of Asian heritage also feel that it indicates a willingness to assimilate to American culture and that an American name can reduce teasing over cultural differences. When deciding on a new name, Yee Ching found that typical American girls' names, like Mary or Sally, did not appeal to her. Her proud father chose the name Flossie, after a recent typhoon, because he believed that his daughter was a force of nature.

The *Lancet* later reported, "It was to prove a fitting name for such a determined and tenacious person."

Quoted in Georgina Kenyon, "Flossie Wong-Staal," *The Lancet: Infectious Diseases*, September 2020. www.thelancet.com.

proof that the human T-lymphotropic virus type 1 (HTLV-1) causes cancer, which contributed to the understanding of how cancers function, even those not caused by viruses. At the time, retroviruses were a relatively new area of study. Prior to Gallo's discovery of HTLV-1, they had only been observed in animals such as mice and birds, never humans. Retroviruses invade cells by inserting their genes into the DNA of their human or animal host, which makes them complicated to treat.

What Gallo and Wong-Staal had learned about retroviruses from their study of HTLV-1 soon proved to be key in studying a new disease. In the early 1980s American doctors began to recognize an influx of cases of rare lung infections and a rare and aggressive cancer, Kaposi's sarcoma, among gay men. These opportunistic infections and others were usually only seen in individuals with weakened immune systems. Doctors were confused, because many of these individuals had been healthy prior to the infections. By the end of 1981, there were 337 reported cases of individuals with a similar immune deficiency, including female patients, children, and infants. By the end of 1981, 130 of these patients had died. The high death rate caused what now is known to be human immunodeficiency virus (HIV) to become a public health crisis in the United States. Both fear and misinformation were rampant among the general public.

Wong-Staal and Gallo hypothesized that this mystery disease might also be a retrovirus. It was transmitted by blood and infected white blood cells known as T cells, just as the HTLV-1 retrovirus was. Wong-Staal and her lab pivoted to trying to find the virus that was causing the disease. With this knowledge, researchers could then try to determine options both to diagnose and treat the mystery disease. Wong-Staal later reflected on this early work: “We need[ed] to understand what the virus is at the molecular level. And as it turns out, the virus was very compli-

Wong-Staal had a prolific partnership with Robert Gallo, pictured here.

cated, so we had to identify each gene. . . . It's a very interesting and complicated virus. So that means that there's a lot of discovery to be made. . . . That was a very productive period. I mean, it's sort of dizzying, you know, because there's so much to do."[20]

Scientists knew nothing about HIV at the time, but groups all over the world were working hard to identify this mysterious virus. In 1983 Wong-Staal's group of researchers, a team in France and a team in San Francisco, all were able to identify the virus. Wong-Staal and her fellow researchers are credited with the discovery that the illness known as acquired immunodeficiency syndrome (AIDS) is caused by HIV.

Her most influential research on HIV came two years later in 1985, when her team successfully cloned the virus. This work was key to developing tests that could screen blood, such as donations at blood banks, for HIV. Unraveling the complications of the AIDS virus meant progress toward treatment and hope for those who contracted the disease. Wong-Staal referred to her study of the virus as akin to "putting your hand in a treasure chest. Every time you put your hand in, you pull out a gem."[21] Wong-Staal found that the HIV virus was constantly mutating, a discovery that would prove critical to developing the antiviral drug cocktails that would help manage the symptoms of AIDS. This knowledge of the fundamental molecular biology of HIV also helped with the creation of a blood test that could detect the virus by its genome rather than viral antibodies, which meant that doctors could diagnose AIDS in patients. "Her groundbreaking work on the molecular biology of HIV inspired scientists worldwide to join the field of human retrovirology, an entirely uncharted but increasingly exciting area of research in the 1980s and early 1990s,"[22] says Genoveffa Franchini, a past postdoctoral fellow in Wong-Staal's NIH lab.

"Her groundbreaking work on the molecular biology of HIV inspired scientists world-wide to join the field of human retrovirology, an entirely uncharted but increasingly exciting area of research in the 1980s and early 1990s."[22]

—Genoveffa Franchini, past postdoctoral fellow in Wong-Staal's lab

Persistence and Further Research

In 1990, after seventeen years at the NIH lab, Wong-Staal decided it was time for a change. She felt like her contributions to AIDS and other research were undervalued and was ready to have the autonomy of running her own lab. She decided to return to UCSD as the Florence Seeley Riford Chair in AIDS Research. She was excited about the opportunity to work with the youth and energy that students provided and told *The Scientist* that a key part of her research would be "understanding how the AIDS virus works by focusing on regulation . . . [and] apply[ing] that technique and approach to vaccine development."[23]

In her new role, Wong-Staal struggled to obtain grants to fund her research. But this was not a barrier to her, as Franchini remembers:

> When she submitted her first grant application from UCSD after leaving the NIH, the reviewers did not give her a fundable score because they thought that, as a molecular biologist, she did not have the immunology experience required to carry out the proposed studies. In response, she conducted the study anyway, published the data, and sent the publication with her next grant application.[24]

Wong-Staal's tenacity and performance impressed her superiors at UCSD, and she was named as the director of both the newly formed Center for AIDS Research and the AIDS Research Institute.

Wong-Staal began her research at UCSD by exploring avenues to treat and perhaps even prevent HIV. She experimented with gene therapy using stem cells in an attempt to suppress the HIV virus by preventing it from reproducing. Gene therapy continues to be used to treat patients diagnosed with HIV to manage symptoms and prevent the development of opportunistic infections. These treatments have resulted in HIV no longer being a death sentence, as it often was during the early days of the AIDS epidemic. Wong-Staal also studied the Tat protein present in Kaposi's sarcoma lesions, which most commonly occur in patients diagnosed with AIDS, and discovered a correlation between the amount of the protein present and how many lesions a patient had. Her findings helped develop new treatments for the lesions. While Wong-Staal's discoveries were important to the study of the HIV virus, they also proved to have applications to other diseases. "AIDS research has been very beneficial to basic research," Wong-Staal said in a 1997 interview. "I mean, from this model, this system, you know, we gain a lot of insights on basic molecular biology and virology and immunology."[25]

Wong-Staal completed important work on HIV/AIDS. Here she addresses a session of the 10th International Conference on AIDS in Yokohama, Japan, in 1994.

Her interest in finding treatments for diseases beyond AIDS also led her into the private sector. Wong-Staal became interested in studying hepatitis C and recognized the need for new drugs to treat the disease. Even after she retired, Wong-Staal still served in an advisory capacity and as a research professor of medicine at UCSD.

In 2019 Wong-Staal received the honor of being inducted for her contributions in the study of HIV into the National Women's Hall of Fame, which honors American women's contributions to our society in the arts, science, and more.

The next year, on July 8, 2020, Wong-Staal died of pneumonia during the height of the COVID-19 pandemic. Her research laid the foundation for scientists to understand diseases like COVID-19 and develop treatments for them. Jerome Zack, a UCLA microbiology, immunology, and molecular genetics professor, believes that her work now informs his research in pathogenesis, which is the study of the progression of diseases and disorders. "Her molecular analysis of HIV influenced how

Why Is There No Vaccine for HIV?

There are some diseases—such as diphtheria, polio, and smallpox—that have been mostly eradicated since the introduction of vaccines. So why has a similar vaccine not been developed for HIV? One of Wong-Staal's key discoveries about the HIV virus was that it was constantly mutating. So even if the proper antibodies were developed for a vaccine, the virus would simply change to escape the antibodies. There are also many subgroups, known as clads, of HIV, which means that even if a vaccine for a certain clad could be developed, it would likely not be effective against other clads. The nature of the virus itself also makes the vaccine method of using live virus, usually considered more effective than vaccines using inactivated virus, extremely risky. The HIV virus integrates itself into its human host's DNA, which means that using a live vaccine virus actually could cause the person to develop AIDS rather than preventing it. While there is a continued interest in developing an HIV vaccine, the constraints of the virus itself and technological limitations mean that it is unlikely to happen in the near future.

virologists study viruses today, such as COVID-19, and the development of antiretroviral drugs," Zack said after her death. "Antiretroviral drugs halt the progression of retroviruses, a type of virus that reproduces by inserting its genetic material into the body's cells."[26] Her younger daughter, Caroline Vega, remembered a dedicated, confident, and persistent scientist who earned the respect of those she worked with, saying, "I have this memory of her in a lab coat surrounded by men, all who were much taller. She was only 5 foot 2. But she always had a commanding presence."[27]

"I have this memory of her in a lab coat surrounded by men, all who were much taller. She was only 5 foot 2. But she always had a commanding presence."[27]

—Caroline Vega, Wong-Staal's daughter

Jenny Han, Author

Jenny Han makes her living by writing books and screenplays for young adults, and she recalls that as a child and teenager, it was reading that sustained her. "I would gobble them up,"[28] she says about her favorite reads as a child, which included *The Baby-Sitters Club* series by Ann M. Martin and books by Judy Blume and Lois Lowry. *Just as Long as We're Together* by Judy Blume was one of the only young adult novels Jenny read with an Asian American girl character. Jenny spent most days after school at the local public library, where the school bus would drop her after school, and read through the middle grade and young adult sections of the library until her mother picked her up to go home. And she did not read only in the library. Han says, "I would read in the bathtub, the dinner table, the car. Whatever I had access to."[29]

Growing Up a Reader and Writer

Jenny Han was born on September 3, 1980, in the Richmond, Virginia, suburb of Chesterfield to South Korean immigrant parents. In the suburban neighborhood where she grew up, her family was one of the few of Asian descent, but many extended family members had settled nearby in the Richmond area. She grew up spending time with her aunts, uncles, and cousins, and for a period of her childhood her grandparents lived with her, her parents, and her younger sister. She formed a close relationship with her grandfather. Sometimes being the child of immigrant parents was challenging. "As a child of immigrants, I did have a lot more responsibilities," Han later reflected. "I had to help my parents with language or culture, so I was used to being in that role."[30]

"As a child of immigrants, I did have a lot more responsibilities. I had to help my parents with language or culture, so I was used to being in that role."[30]

—Jenny Han

At home, her mother was a bit of the stereotypical Asian mom, Han says, demanding hard work. "My mom forced both my little sister and me to take piano lessons, we did math flashcards at night, we went to Korean school every Saturday morning. But both of my parents have always been incredibly supportive of my writing and of creativity in general. My sister loved to swim, I loved to read—whatever we had a passion for, my parents supported."[31]

Jenny Han says that as a child, reading sustained her. The Baby-Sitters Club *was a favorite series of hers.*

Jenny's love of writing also developed when she was a child, when she began writing stories that won classroom prizes. Now Han is amused that as an elementary student, her stories featured characters with leukemia and with divorcing parents, since she had no experience with either. The schools Jenny attended were not diverse, and this experience of constantly feeling different took a toll, especially during middle school. For high school, Jenny attended a local magnet school and finally felt like she belonged. Han said in 2020 about her high school experience, "It was a really diverse school. . . . I just learned so much about other cultures that I never would have known about if I had stayed in my regular school."[32]

Becoming an Author

Although Han grew up with writing as one of her favorite pastimes, before college she had not considered becoming an author. "I never saw any writers. I . . . certainly didn't see any young writers or Asian-American female writers," Han later said of her career ambitions. "So it never seemed like something within my reach."[33] That changed when she went to the University of North Carolina and took a Writing for Children workshop. She gravitated toward writing for young adults and children, the age group that she most identified with, being just out of her teens herself. At the time, there were few true young adult books. As Han commented about her own reading as a child, "You kind of went from 'Baby-Sitters Club' books to Stephen King. There wasn't as much in the middle."[34]

As she wound down her undergraduate experience at the University of North Carolina, Han knew that she wanted to get a job that somehow involved children's books, whether writing them, publishing them, or teaching about them. She applied to graduate programs in teaching and writing. Ultimately, she chose to study writing. She later said of that decision, "I knew there was more security in a teaching degree, but I couldn't let go of my writing dream either. Besides, I've always been a gambling woman by nature. I was 22. I figured if it didn't work out, I'd have

Writing Asian American Characters

Han has been asked in interviews why she chose to have White protagonists in her first middle grade novel, *Shug*, and in *The Summer I Turned Pretty* series instead of featuring Asian American main characters. About *Shug*, Han has said that she simply imagined her main character as a skinny girl on the cusp of puberty who just happened to be White. But she also acknowledges that featuring Asian American main characters presents a challenge. "In children's books, if your character was the person of color, then it was going to be a book about some sort of problem, some historical issue," she says of the expectations from publishers. "So if I'm Asian, then the issue would be Japanese internment camps. Or it was going to be a story about being sad that my parents were really strict." Her chapter book for young elementary students, *Clara Lee and the Apple Pie Dream*, was released in 2011 and was the first of hers to feature an Asian American main character. The book is based on Han's own close relationship with her grandfather and her younger sister. It also explores Clara Lee's complicated relationship with her Korean heritage and culture.

Quoted in Rachel Seo, "'Anyone Could Be the Girl Next Door': How Jenny Han Defied Hollywood Typecasting to Turn 'The Summer I Turned Pretty' into a Smash Hit," *Variety*, July 28, 2023. https://variety.com.

the rest of my life to pay off loans. Grown-ups spend that much on cars, why not make an investment on my future?"[35]

Han graduated with a master of fine arts in writing for children in 2006, the same year her first novel, the middle grade book *Shug*, was published. Han insisted that the book feature her headshot on the back flap, something that was not traditionally done at the time, because she was so proud of her achievement of becoming a published author.

Initially, Han was unable to make a living solely from her writing, so she continued to work full time, both as a bookseller and in a school library. Working with children and teens provided inspiration for her writing and gave her insight into what was popular with them. She also found inspiration in the vibrant, busy life

"I knew there was more security in a teaching degree, but I couldn't let go of my writing dream either. . . . I figured if it didn't work out, I'd have the rest of my life to pay off loans."[35]

—Jenny Han

of New York City, where she decided to stay after graduate school. "Sometimes it'll be something as random as being on the subway and then the thought just like pops into my head or somebody walks by and I think that I should put something like that in my book,"[36] Han said in 2016 about developing ideas for her books.

A Bestselling Author

Success took time, but in 2009 the first novel of Han's *The Summer I Turned Pretty* trilogy was published, with the second and third coming out in 2010 and 2011. This series catapulted Han into being a bestselling author, with teen readers clamoring for more books from her. *The Summer I Turned Pretty* series offered what appealed to teens: friendship, self-discovery, and the giddy experience of falling in love for the first time. "When you're young, you don't have a lot of control over even basic things in your life. . . . That can feel sort of unstable in its own way," says Han about writing for young adults. "And that's why I like writing about that time. . . . I think there's a tenderness that we have toward the story, but also toward our readers."[37]

The popularity of *The Summer I Turned Pretty* books led Han to decide that her next young adult books would feature an Asian American main character. The *To All the Boys I've Loved Before* books, featuring Lara Jean Song Covey, were released in 2014, 2015, and 2017. It was important for Han that Lara Jean's Asian American heritage be part of who she was but not be the focus of the series. "What I've wanted and pushed for was just having more options for people," Han says, "If you want to go to the beach and read something, you could read a romantic story with a person of color and still have the light and fun story. . . . Anyone could be the girl next door."[38] Han based the character of Lara Jean on her own teen years as an Asian American high schooler in Virginia.

American teens loved Han's girl next door Lara Jean, and the books all spent time on the *New York Times* bestseller list, the first for forty weeks. The series was eventually translated into thirty different languages. The first in the trilogy was also the first on the

The Summer I Turned Pretty ***catapulted Han into success. The book was later turned into a Netflix series. She is pictured here with her family at the 2022 premiere.***

New York Times bestseller list ever to feature an Asian girl on the cover. That cover was important to Han. "I said from the get-go that I wanted the art to be photographic so that I could see an Asian girl on a book cover," Han said in an interview with *Teen Vogue*. "I had this image in my mind of an Asian-American girl walking into a bookstore, seeing Lara Jean, and feeling recognized and seen."[39]

To Hollywood

Han's bestsellers soon attracted the attention of those interested in adapting them for the screen. First the *To All the Boys I've Loved Before* trilogy was adapted into three movies by Netflix, with the first coming out in 2018. While the producers asked for feedback from Han, she was not involved in the screenwriting or producing of the films. The process to get the first film made was long and rather overwhelming for Han because she was trust-

Fighting for Representation

Han has always gotten pushback from both the publishing and TV/film industry for writing stories featuring Asian American characters. Publishers told her during her early career that readers would not be interested in stories about Asian American families and that such stories did not sell. Even with the bestselling trilogy of *To All the Boys I've Loved Before* featuring a Korean American main character proving that they do indeed sell, during the adaptation to film, Han faced the same problem. "Something I came up against in Hollywood was, 'Why does she have to be Asian?' It's like: 'That's just who she is!' I'm hoping that with the more representation we have, it's less about there having to be some sort of big reason for it," she says. A barrier to featuring actors of Asian American heritage is also that producers want big names, which is challenging since actors of color, especially Asian American actors, are underrepresented. Han hopes that continuing to feature Asian American actors in her films and TV shows will lead to more opportunities and representation in Hollywood for actors of color, as well as those of different sizes and sexual identities.

Quoted in Paula Peters Chambers, "Young at Heart," *En Forme*, November 30, 2021. https://enformeva.com.

ing the producers and screenwriter with her stories. But in the end, it was a movie that she, and the readers of the trilogy, were pleased with, and it ended up attracting many more fans to her work as well. The response to the release of the movie was also overwhelming: there were 85 million views just in the first month.

Several months after the *To All the Boys I've Loved Before* release, Netflix announced that it had been one of its most popular original films, with many repeat viewers. It also created what *Publishers Weekly* dubbed the Han effect, the increase in desire in the publishing industry for emotionally rich young adult romantic comedies that appealed to both teens and adults. For Han, the most meaningful result of the films has been its impact on young women, especially Asian American teens. The October following the release of the first movie, Han was brought to tears when she started seeing all the pictures of girls dressed up as Lara Jean for Halloween. Several months later, she reflected on viewing them:

They started to pour in, picture after picture. To be able to see this character, Lara Jean, take her place in the pantheon of Asian American female characters of which there are so few. Halloween is limited when you're trying to think of a character to be from pop culture. The options are so limited. To think there's one more option where someone can say, "there's someone who looks like me and I can emulate," is profoundly moving.[40]

The popularity of Han's movie trilogy on Netflix caused renewed interest in her original trilogy, *The Summer I Turned Pretty*. Book sales spiked, and so did interest in also adapting the series

This photo shows Han at the premiere of To All the Boys P.S. I Still Love You, *which was one of Netflix's most popular original films.*

for film. Han's resulting deal with Amazon Prime to produce the three-season TV series allowed her much more creative control as show creator and showrunner, the executive producer who manages the TV show production and oversees the creative direction it will take.

> **"[An] American girl doesn't look just one kind of way, not in 2018, not ever. That's what I wanted to showcase for the girls who don't fit that mold of what people think an American girl looks like."[42]**
>
> **—Jenny Han**

Han also created her own production banner, Jenny Kissed Me, which she says is centered on "coming of age, at any age."[41] And she signed a longer-term deal with Amazon that included her most recent TV series and the first not based on her books: *XO, Kitty*. Through her works, she continues in her goal of making teens like herself, a girl embracing both her Korean and American sides, feel seen. In 2023 she reflected on the creation of her most popular character:

> The way I conceived of Lara Jean was to be a modern-day children's book heroine, the same kind of heroine I grew up reading, except I never really saw an Asian-American girl be the heroine. . . . [An] American girl doesn't look just one kind of way, not in 2018, not ever. That's what I wanted to showcase for the girls who don't fit that mold of what people think an American girl looks like, but also for the girls who do fit that mold, because I think that representation is good for everybody.[42]

CHAPTER FOUR

Anna Sui, Fashion Designer

Anna Sui's first forays into design were not in creating fashions for the biggest rock stars but in her childhood bedroom. First she had an all-Barbie bedroom, then she says she "headed for hot pink. Even the inside of my closet was pink. I always loved a *complete* environment."[43] In her teens, Anna's bedroom was inspired by Victorian illustrator Aubrey Beardsley, with gray walls and furniture she lacquered black herself. Anna's fashion choices as a girl were inspired by her mother, who made much of her own wardrobe and taught Anna to make her own clothes, shoe covers, and bags with leftover fabric. She also loved browsing through her mother's fashion and movie magazines, looking at pictures of fashion icons such as Jackie Kennedy and Elizabeth Taylor. "There were moments when I would grab onto something and try to find out more about it," Sui later said of her childhood forays into fashion research. "Where did those looks come from? What were the rock stars' wives wearing and what were British designers doing in these boutiques?"[44]

"There were moments when I would grab onto something and try to find out more about it. Where did those looks come from? What were the rock stars' wives wearing and what were British designers doing in these boutiques?"[44]

—Anna Sui

Growing Up Chinese in Michigan

Anna Sui was born on August 4, 1955, to first-generation Chinese American parents Paul Wai Kong Sui and Grace Kwang

Chi Fang. Paul and Grace had immigrated to the United States to escape the 1949 Chinese Communist Revolution. Her family lived in Dearborn, Michigan, and Sui remembers that during her childhood her family was the only Chinese family in town. This made her stand out, but as journalist Ligaya Mishan later wrote, "Sui says she never felt like she was stigmatized for being Chinese, although, [Sui] adds, 'I also didn't accept that stigma.'"[45]

Anna's refusal to adhere to the norms imposed on her began in childhood, when she determined her future career goals after traveling to New York and being the flower girl in the wedding of an aunt and uncle. "When I went back to Michigan," Sui recalled in 2023, "I told my parents, 'When I grow up, I'm going to be a fashion designer and move to New York.'"[46]

Anna Sui was born to first-generation Chinese American parents.

Her parents were less than impressed by her declaration, wanting her to pursue something more practical, like a career as a doctor. However, Sui credits the Chinese cultural focus on boys instead of girls for her parents focusing largely on the interests and ambitions of her older and younger brothers, Bobby and Eddy, and leaving her mostly to her dreams of design and fashion. As she grew older, she and Bobby would head into Detroit on the weekends, visiting boutiques owned by local designers and attending shows by local bands, including the Stooges with Iggy Pop and MC5. She became as fascinated with the music scene as she was with fashion, watching *The Ed Sullivan Show* on television and attending concerts by the Monkees and others.

Reading *Seventeen* magazine as a teen ended up providing the path to New York City when she found an advertisement for Parsons School of Design and sent in for a course catalog. Sui recalls, “From that point on I geared my whole curriculum toward getting into Parsons. New York seemed so far away then. I would go once every summer and would get my one glimpse of what I thought was fashion. I’d visit the Biba boutique at Bergdorf Goodman, and it was the first time I’d ever seen all those incredible colors: dusty rose, charcoal, plum, teal.”[47]

When Sui moved to New York after high school and acceptance to Parsons, reality did not quite measure up to her dreams. The fashion design program turned out to be very elitist, with students even forbidden to eat in the cafeteria because they would be mingling with students in other programs. But Sui did so anyway, which led to her meeting Steven Meisel, who became an iconic fashion photographer. Meisel introduced her to friends in his circle and to the city’s club and music scene. “I was in New York at the most exciting time in the ’70s, seeing all the punk rock fans and going to the Mudd Club,” Sui remembers of that time. “I saw the best of New York and the best of nightlife and the best of music.”[48]

Club Scene, Club Fashion

Spending time with her friends and with the 1970s punk rock musicians in her larger circle—which included the Ramones, the New York Dolls, and David Bowie—led Sui to want to create clothing that was different from the expensive, high-end couture fashion that dominated at Parsons. She wanted to make clothing that her friends would want to wear when they went to the club. "I'd rather pick out a gingham and think, 'How do I make this look like a million bucks?'"[49] she said of her rejection of couture fashion and expensive fabrics at the time. Her unhappiness at Parsons led her to drop out after two years and accept a job with fashion brand Charlie's Girls. Sui also began styling for Meisel's photo shoots. After the closure of Charlie's Girls, Sui had roles designing for several sportswear companies. While much of the clothing being created was for women, the fashion industry was still very male-dominated at that time. "Even when I first started working in the garment center, all my bosses were men. A lot of the designers were men, too," Sui told *Fashion Week Daily* in 2024. "The women were in the background as design assistants who were draping or sewing or making the patterns."[50]

Creating clothing that was not what she wanted to design was frustrating for Sui and even led her to be fired from one job, with her boss telling her that her designs were not right for his company because they did not match the brand's aesthetic. And Sui realized that he was right. "I had to make choices [based on] things that I could do and suited my tastes as opposed to trying to do just anything,"[51] she eventually said about his hurtful remarks. Sui got another job working for a sportswear company, but she also continued to work on her own designs. Then, in 1981, two big department store chains—Macy's and Bloomingdale's—took notice of her work. They bought some of her designs and featured them in window displays and a full-page advertisement in the *New York Times*. Her boss at the sportswear company saw the ad and was not happy about it. He fired her.

A Family Affair

Anna Sui's nieces have turned her brand into a bit of a family affair. As children, they would visit her runway shows in New York Fashion Week and choose their favorite looks. Sui would then create smaller versions of her clothing for them to wear and feature in their own fashion shows. As teens and young adults, her nieces traveled with her on her summer inspiration trips to international locations such as Egypt, India, and Australia. Being immersed in the fashion world from a young age influenced the girls' own career directions. Chase Sui Wonders became a model and actress and has modeled clothing for her aunt. Her sister, Jeannie Sui Wonders, is a filmmaker and photographer who has created short fashion films for the Anna Sui brand. Isabelle Sui, who became Anna Sui's director of operations, says about her aunt, "She's such an inspiration. It's amazing to have such a talented female figure growing up your whole life. It's taught us all to follow our dreams and know we can do whatever we want to do."

Quoted in Eddie Roche, "Anna Sui Reflects on 33 Years in Fashion—and What's Coming Next!," *Fashion Week Daily*, September 9, 2024. https://fashionweekdaily.com.

Although it did not seem like it at the time, being fired (again) turned out to be the best thing that could have happened to Sui. She was now able to focus on her own business while taking on freelance design work to supplement her income. She ran her business out of her downtown New York apartment for ten years. But it was a stressful time as she tried to keep herself and her business financially afloat and pay her employees. "When I had to get a line of credit with the bank, or when I had to do freelance . . . because I had to keep the whole thing going," Sui reflected on the responsibility, "[there were points] here I might not have even had enough money to take the subway, but would walk to the Garment Center and look for fabric or go pick up zippers."[52] The glitz, power suits, huge shoulders, and oversized fits that were popular in the 1980s also were not a fit with Sui's edgy "rocker" yet feminine aesthetic. "There were so many times during the power dressing eighties when I thought of giving up and becoming a stylist because I

> "There were so many times during the power dressing eighties when I thought of giving up and becoming a stylist because I knew I could at least make money."[53]
>
> —Anna Sui

knew I could at least make money,"[53] Sui reflected later of that challenging period.

The pivotal moment when Sui realized she was ready to stage her first runway show came while attending 1990 Paris Fashion Week. "We stopped at the Ritz to pick up Madonna and she had her coat on already," Sui remembers. "When she sat down at the Gaultier show, she took off her coat and said, 'Anna, I have a surprise for you!' She was wearing my babydoll dress."[54]

Friends and connections that she made over the years showed up to help Sui stage her first budget-friendly runway show in 1991 with models Naomi Campbell, Christy Turlington, and Linda Evangelista, among others. The opening of her boutique the following year was also a do-it-yourself collaboration with friends and family. Her brother Eddy help her source rock posters to decorate the shop and to sell. "My friends and I put it all together," said Sui of her Greene Street boutique. "They helped me paint the walls. We made papier-mâché doll heads."[55]

Sui's Influence on the Fashion and Music Industries

Sui's designs were a smash hit with many, especially among those in the fashion industry and with actresses and musicians. The Council of Fashion Designers of America (CFDA) awarded her the New Fashion Talent Award in 1992. Sui remembers of that night, "All of a sudden, I heard these heels clicking and running after me. I turned around and it was Barbra Streisand and Donna Karan. Barb was like, 'Anna, Anna, where can I get your clothes?'"[56] In 2009 Sui was awarded the CFDA Geoffrey Beene Lifetime Achievement Award.

In the early days of her label, she took inspiration from the music industry, and soon musicians were wearing her garments onstage, at awards shows, and elsewhere. Unlike some of her contemporaries, who were creating clothing that often was not embraced off the runway, Sui's clothing was designed to be

Sui is interviewed in her New York office in 2005. She likes to push boundaries and mix patterns and textures in interesting ways.

worn and enjoyed, whether by a rock star onstage or by a young woman going out for a night on the town. Journalist Ligaya Mishan believes that her clothing continues to resonate because it is accessible and represents "the archetypal American teen, the one who, in her bedroom, is trying on different selves—hippie, preppy, punk, wild child and free spirit—rebirthing herself again and again. . . .The clothes she makes aren't totems of some inaccessibly glamorous life but an invitation: to join the party, to be one of those girls."[57]

Sui delights in pushing boundaries in both her runway shows and designs. She mixes fabrics, like leather and lace, enjoying combinations of hard and soft, the edgy and the feminine. Patterns and textures are mixed in interesting ways, and inspiration is taken from vintage clothing and music trends such as 1960s mod and 1970s punk. While Marc Jacobs, designing for cloth-

> **"You can have the best sound engineer on the planet, but no matter how high you crank up an amp, a good outfit still hits the loudest onstage. It's just as true for Olivia Rodrigo's princess-core prom wrecks . . . and Madonna's black baptism dresses from her *Like a Prayer* era."[59]**
>
> —Faran Krentcil, fashion journalist

ing company Perry Ellis, is often credited for the emergence of grunge as a fashion trend inspired by grunge musicians, Sui released a grunge collection the same season, in the spring of 1993. That show also debuted her first menswear collection. Mick Jagger was her first customer for the line. Embracing androgyny and blurred lines between what defines menswear and women's wear is also something that Sui has explored. "Androgyny is a permanent fixture in rock music. . . . Dyed hair, eye makeup, lamé, velvet, ruffles, high-heeled boots," Sui said about her choice to explore androgyny in her designs. "Fashion is like rock in that ambiguity is one of its stocks in trade."[58] In 1997 she sent Dave Navarro, guitarist for the Red Hot Chili Peppers, down the runway in lingerie and leather pants.

Today's Stars in Anna Sui

Anna Sui may have been designing for over thirty years, but her creations are far from old-fashioned or irrelevant. In fact, many of today's Gen Z stars are seen out and about in her designs. In her collections she takes inspiration both from vintage looks and what her twenty-something nieces enjoy wearing. Some of the young stars who wear her clothing are Olivia Rodrigo, Ariana Grande, Suki Waterhouse, Dua Lipa, and Zendaya. Sui says of Rodrigo:

> I think she's amazing and [has] like the most incredible style. I think it's her style and not somebody telling her, "Wear this; wear that." And you can see that her personality matches the way she looks. I think she's very true to herself, so I was really flattered when I saw that she started wearing my pieces! I love to see a mix of the old stuff and the new, too. It's great to know that girls are still dressing the way we used to do it when we were just out of school.

Quoted in Faran Krentcil, "How Anna Sui Created Some of Music's Most Iconic Looks," Alternative Press, April 13, 2023. www.altpress.com.

A woman looks at an exhibition in honor of Sui at the Museum of Art and Design at Central Park in Manhattan.

Sui's longevity in the New York fashion world is partially due to her skills in bargaining licensing deals that have created an Anna Sui empire of perfumes and cosmetics in addition to her clothing. But fashion journalist Faran Krentcil believes her continuing popularity also stems from her skill in creating iconic looks for musicians:

> You can have the best sound engineer on the planet, but no matter how high you crank up an amp, a good outfit still hits the loudest onstage. It's just as true for Olivia Rodrigo's princess-core prom wrecks as it is for Dave Navarro's leather-and-lingerie combos circa *Blood Sugar Sex Magic*, and Madonna's black baptism dresses from her *Like a Prayer* era. And behind the seams of all those looks? It's Anna Sui.[59]

From 2017 to 2022 a retrospective of Anna Sui's thirty years of design traveled the world with over one hundred garments representing all the different archetypes that Sui has explored over the years, from rock star to punk, offering a look into her creative process.

Mindy Kaling, Actor

At age fourteen, Mindy Kaling had a friend she defined as a "Saturday friend," whom she hung out with on the weekends but not at school. She and Mavis shared a love of comedy and would spend hours on Saturdays watching Comedy Central and laughing together. "We'd start with the good shows, *Dr. Katz*, *Kids in the Hall*, or *Saturday Night Live* reruns," Kaling wrote in her first memoir, "[and then on to our least] favorite programming, but like the tray of croissants from Costco my mom left for us on the kitchen table, Mavis and I devoured it nonetheless."[60] Then the reenactments of the funniest moments they saw would occur, at least until Kaling's mother would beg her to stop repeating catchphrases in annoying voices. But in those comedy shows and elsewhere on-screen she did not see any Asian American women or girls. "You cannot imagine how excited I was when *Bend It like Beckham* came out." Kaling says of seeing the movie, "The idea that I could actually see people from my community onscreen blew my mind."[61]

> **"You cannot imagine how excited I was when *Bend It like Beckham* came out. The idea that I could actually see people from my community onscreen blew my mind."[61]**
>
> **—Mindy Kaling**

Missing On-Screen

Mindy Kaling was born Vera Mindy Chokalingam on June 24, 1979, in Cambridge, Massachusetts, the second child of parents Avudaiappan Chokalingam and Swati Chokalingam. Her parents were immigrants from India, her father an architect and mother an obstetrician/gynecologist. While growing up, she was very close to her mother, and as an adult she reflected, "The best relationship I had in my life was the one with my mom. It was so pure and so fun and uncomplicated, and I hope that I can have that with my son or daughter—if I'm lucky, with at least one of my kids—when they get older."[62] Mindy felt both inspired by her driven parents and accepted by them, even in spite of her weight, as she was a self-proclaimed chubby child.

Mindy Kaling was excited to see the movie, Bend It like Beckham, *because it was a rare opportunity to watch people from her community onscreen.*

While growing up, Mindy always felt awkward, overlooked, and rather average, especially in school. Her struggles with eating, dieting, and being bullied for being overweight would follow her through her childhood and teen years. Anything athletic was challenging for her. She developed a hatred for bike riding and worried about embarrassing her older brother at summer camp when she was scared of jumping off the diving board. Kaling describes herself as a classic nerd during high school—the girl with crushes but no boyfriends. Her interest in acting and comedy bled into school, where she tried out for school plays. "They cast the same popular, pretty people over and over while I played a hobo or a homeless woman for, like, nine consecutive productions," Kaling reflected in 2015 on never getting a meaningful role. "That was really hard. I had such an inherent trust in adults that all I could think was: This must mean I'm actually really bad at this."[63]

After she graduated from high school and majored in theater at Dartmouth College, the feelings of being excluded and overlooked began to fade. Kaling began taking creative writing classes and found that her high school experiences actually were valuable. She recalls, "Because I was largely overlooked at school, I watched everyone like an observant weirdo. . . . It has helped me so much as a writer; you have no idea."[64] She joined an improv group, wrote and performed in student productions, sang, and even worked as a cartoonist for the student newspaper. "I finally got to do and express what I was passionate about," Kaling says about her college experience. "The best part? People thought I was funny, and that gave me confidence and made me try more stuff, which made me funnier!"[65] This period of trying everything included a summer internship at *Late Night with Conan O'Brien*.

Breaking into the Industry

After graduating from Dartmouth College in 2001, Kaling and two friends moved to New York City. None of them had jobs yet, and they settled into a tiny walk-up apartment in Brooklyn. Kaling pur-

How Kaling's Parents Appear in Her Work

While Mindy Kaling's parents have undoubtedly inspired her work ethic and drive, they have also appeared in her work in other ways. In the "Diwali" episode she wrote for *The Office*, her character Kelly's parents are played by Kaling's actual parents. "We only cast my parents in it . . . because we had auditioned the parts and Greg felt that the actors we found . . . were either too theatrical for the style of acting on our show, or too stilted, because they had no acting experience," Kaling remembers of the casting. "Now, I'm the first to say that my parents' acting was also very stilted, but [Greg Daniels] was like, 'At least they bear some familial resemblance to you, so we'll put them in there." The director actually loved her father's acting enough to ask whether her parents would come back for another episode, but Kaling declined because she was afraid it might be seen as unprofessional. Later, when Kaling was running her own show, *The Mindy Project*, her character was based on her mother, who sadly had passed away from cancer months before the show premiered.

Quoted in Nicole Gallucci, "Mindy Kaling Talks TV Representation and the 'Diwali' Episode of 'The Office,'" July 1, 2020. Mashable. www.mashable.com.

sued writing for television but soon found that breaking into the industry was going to be a lot harder than she originally thought. She reached out to the producers of *Late Night*, where she had interned during college, and was told they only took submissions from writers with agents. She wrote and submitted a TV script that also generated no interest. The one acting audition she had in that period ended after a disastrous dance audition. After three months, Kaling knew she had to get a job doing something to pay her portion of the rent, and so she started babysitting. However, the money was not actually paying her bills, and she did not even have health insurance. She began interviewing for entry-level network jobs and ended up landing a production assistant job with *Crossing Over with John Edward*. "Working for a TV psychic was not what my parents had envisioned after investing in my degree, but the job had health benefits," Kaling says in her memoir. "I was working at a job that was vaguely in the world of television making $500 a week! Cue Madonna's 'Holiday'!"[66]

She and her friends had few creative outlets in their day jobs, so Kaling and one of her roommates, Brenda Withers, began setting aside time for writing each day. They created two characters, Ben and Matt, loosely based on actors Ben Affleck and Matt Damon, and ended up with a ridiculous short play called *Matt & Ben*. In 2002 they entered it in the New York International Fringe Festival. Kaling later wrote of that production:

> We didn't want to pay a director to direct the show, so Bren and I directed it ourselves. It was a given that we would also star in it, not just because it was fun, but because, again, we didn't want to pay anyone. . . . The set was minimal and we wore guy's clothes that we had borrowed. . . . We had no idea what we were doing, but we had a *purpose* after two years living in New York and not having one.[67]

It may have been a budget production, but the audiences loved it, and *Matt & Ben* was named the best play out of the five hundred shows performed. And then producers wanted to take the play off-Broadway, where it eventually ran for three shows a night. Kaling and Withers's agent was eventually able to leverage this success into a pilot for a sitcom, *Mindy and Brenda*, based on their life living together in New York City.

The Move to Los Angeles

Once Kaling and Withers had moved to Los Angeles to produce their pilot, what they were creating did not feel right anymore: conventionally pretty women were cast to play their parts, and the show did not even feel like it was really about them. Kaling was relieved when the pilot was not picked up by a network to produce. However, while in Los Angeles, she had secured another opportunity: writing for the TV comedy *The Office*. The show's creator Greg Daniels had seen her in *Matt & Ben* and hired her to write six episodes in keeping with NBC's diversity program. "It used to really embarrass me because I thought I had the scarlet letter on me," Kaling recalls.

"'Diversity hire' inherently meant, 'less talented but fulfilling that quota.'"[68]

> **"It used to really embarrass me because I thought I had the scarlet letter on me. 'Diversity hire' inherently meant, 'less talented but fulfilling that quota.'"[68]**
>
> **—Mindy Kaling**

But Kaling's time on *The Office* was far from over after those first six episodes. She went on to write twenty-four episodes for the show, in addition to producing and directing. The character Kelly Kapoor was also created for Kaling, offering an opportunity for a South Asian character who was not a racist caricature to finally appear on prime time television. Especially impactful was the episode titled "Diwali," which was written by Kaling. It was the first time that the holiday was ever featured on an American comedy show. "I had to kind of confront the fact that I'm Indian-American, I don't know very much about the holiday," Kaling said about the episode years later. "Talking about how you don't know very much about the holiday kind of became a big part of the episode, which I loved."[69]

While she was making her mark on the set and on-screen in *The Office*, Kaling was still experiencing sexism in the industry.

Kaling wrote, produced, and directed for The Office*, and the character Kelly Kapoor was created for her. The cast of* The Office *is shown here.*

Thoughts on *Never Have I Ever's* Representation of Indian Culture

For those with Indian heritage, especially young women, *Never Have I Ever* felt like one of the first positive and accurate portrayals of South Asian culture on TV. Before this show, Indian characters were mostly caricatures built around stereotypes. Or they were featured as sidekicks rather than main characters. Faiza Hirji, a professor of communication and media arts, reflects on Devi, the main character in *Never Have I Ever*:

> Devi doesn't just happen to be brown. It's a significant part of her identity, and part of her coming-of-age, coming-to-terms-with-herself story. And yet, her brownness is not the entirety of who she is. She is a rebellious teen who chafes at her mother's strict rules, misses her father, can be self-centered in the way of teenagers, uses some of her prayers to ask earnestly for a thinning of her arm hair. . . . She drives the narrative, and in ways that are alternately inspiring, cringe-worthy and relatable.

Faiza Hirji, "Mindy Kaling's *Never Have I Ever* Makes Me Feel Hopeful About Representation, Gender and Race," The Conversation, May 25, 2020. https://theconversation.com.

When the show received an Emmy nomination, she, the only female producer, was originally told she was not eligible. "They made me, not any of the other producers, fill out a whole form and write an essay about all my contributions as a writer and a producer," Kaling says of the experience. "I had to get letters from all the other male, white producers saying that I had contributed when my actual record stood for itself."[70]

Making Her Mark in Hollywood

After nine seasons on *The Office*, in 2012 Kaling left to produce her own show, *The Mindy Project*, which ran for six seasons, first on Fox and then Hulu. She was the first woman of color to create, write, and star in a network TV show, but she was subject to heavy criticism for how she chose to represent her Indian American main character. In a 2020 *Vogue India* article, she reflected on her decision not to center on her Indian ethnicity: "For a lot of white executives at the TV networks, they kind of wanted it to be [ethnicity driven]. They felt more comfortable with it being about an Indian woman who felt out of place in America educating white people. And it's not that I haven't felt out of place in America as a dark-skinned Indian woman, but it was not the most interesting thing."[71]

Kaling has also commented on several occasions that women of color serving as showrunners, executive producers who are in charge of running all the elements of a TV show, are subject to more scrutiny and are expected to have more diverse casts, while White showrunners and producers are not expected to do so. Kaling later explored some of her experiences surrounding working in the industry as a woman of color in the movie *Late Night*, released

This photo shows Kaling at the premiere for the third season of the Netflix TV show, Never Have I Ever, *whose main character is loosely based on Kaling herself as a teen.*

> **"Coming to terms with my 'Indian-ness' is a big part of the show. . . . Culturally I always felt I straddled the lines of two cultures. Having a daughter really made me look at my faith and culture in a new way because I really want her to identify as Indian."[73]**
>
> —Mindy Kaling

in 2019, which she wrote, produced, and acted in. The film also explores the gender pay gap, diversity, and ageism. Before *Late Night* Kaling also starred in movies such as *Ocean's 8* and *A Wrinkle in Time* and was a voice actor in movies such as *Inside Out*.

Kaling also produced the remake of the movie *Four Weddings and a Funeral* into a TV miniseries in 2019. She found it was the ideal opportunity to feature stories of men and women of color instead of the exclusively White characters featured in the original film. "There's so many great, underrepresented people in London that the movie—which is so amazing—didn't necessarily have the opportunity to show the stories of," says Kaling of this choice. "Doing an adaptation of that through the lens of a British-Pakistani man falling in love with an African-American woman felt interesting to me."[72]

The next year the first season of her teen-centric Netflix TV show, *Never Have I Ever*, was released, featuring the smart and spunky fifteen-year-old Devi, who is loosely based on Kaling herself as a teen. In the show, Devi grapples with being a child of immigrants and her connection with her Indian roots and Hindu traditions, while navigating the typical teenage angst of crushes and school. "Coming to terms with my 'Indian-ness' is a big part of the show," says Kaling of how the show and her life intersect. "Culturally I always felt I straddled the lines of two cultures. Having a daughter really made me look at my faith and culture in a new way because I really want her to identify as Indian."[73]

Now Kaling is producing and writing more than acting. She is focused on producing stories of characters of Indian heritage and creating opportunities for creative women from all different backgrounds. "Especially during these new shows, I realized that the only way that people will have these kinds of opportunities . . . is if people like me make a difference," says Kaling. "We have to be the ones to open the doors for other people."[74]

SOURCE NOTES

Introduction: Leading the Way

1. Quoted in John Yang and Henry Zahn, "Remembering Kalpana Chawla, the First Indian American to Go to Space," *PBS NewsHour*, May 14, 2023. www.pbs.org.
2. Quoted in Sandhya Ramesh, "Karnal to Cosmos & Beyond—Kalpana Chawla's Journey Is Still a Roadmap for India's Dreamers," *The Print*, February 1, 2024. https://theprint.in.
3. Quoted in Leonard D. Chan and Philip Chin, "An Interview with Ibuki Hibi Lee," *AACP Newsletter*, July 2005. www.asianamericanbooks.com.
4. Quoted in Melissa Ho, "Hisako Hibi: An Interview with Curator Melissa Ho," Smithsonian American Women's History Museum. www.becomingvisible.si.edu.

Chapter One: Patsy Mink, US Representative

5. Quoted in Richard Mertens, "Political Pioneer," *University of Chicago Magazine*, September/October 2012. https://mag.uchicago.edu.
6. Quoted in Sophia Smith Collection, "Oral History Interview with Patsy T. Mink," Smith College Special Collections, 1979. https://libraries.smith.edu.
7. Quoted in Mertens, "Political Pioneer."
8. Quoted in Tania Cruz and Eric K. Yamamoto, "A Tribute to Patsy Takemoto Mink," *Asian-Pacific Law & Policy Journal*, Summer 2003, p. 577.
9. Quoted in Cruz and Yamamoto, "A Tribute to Patsy Takemoto Mink," p. 579.
10. Quoted in Mertens, "Political Pioneer."
11. Quoted in Honolulu Advertiser, "Hawai'i, Nation Lose 'a Powerful Voice,'" September 29, 2002. https://the.honoluluadvertiser.com.
12. Quoted in Cruz and Yamamoto, "A Tribute to Patsy Takemoto Mink," p. 585.
13. Quoted in Mertens, "Political Pioneer."
14. Quoted in Mertens, "Political Pioneer."
15. Quoted in US Department of Education, "Title IX and Sex Discrimination." www.ed.gov.
16. Quoted in Honolulu Advertiser, "Hawai'i, Nation Lose 'a Powerful Voice.'"

Chapter Two: Flossie Wong-Staal, Scientist

17. Quoted in Victoria Harde and Caroline Hannaway, "Oral History Interview with Dr. Flossie Wong-Staal on the National Institutes of Health's Response to AIDS," Office of NIH History, December 10, 1997. https://m.moam.info.

18. Quoted in Harde and Hannaway, "Oral History Interview with Dr. Flossie Wong-Staal on the National Institutes of Health's Response to AIDS."
19. Quoted in National Cancer Institute Center for Cancer Research, "In Memoriam: Flossie Wong-Staal, Ph.D.," July 13, 2020. https://ccr.cancer.gov.
20. Quoted in Harde and Hannaway, "Oral History Interview with Dr. Flossie Wong-Staal on the National Institutes of Health's Response to AIDS."
21. Quoted in Bill Branson, "Flossie Wong-Staal, Who Unlocked Mystery of H.I.V., Dies at 73," *New York Times*, July 17, 2020. www.nytimes.com.
22. Genoveffa Franchini, "Flossie Wong-Staal (1946–2020): Trailblazing HIV Researcher," *Science*, September 11, 2020. www.science.org.
23. Quoted in *The Scientist*, "Leading AIDS Researcher Chosen for New Chair at UC-San Diego," February 18, 1990. www.the-scientist.com.
24. Franchini, "Flossie Wong-Staal (1946–2020)."
25. Quoted in Harde and Hannaway, "Oral History Interview with Dr. Flossie Wong-Staal on the National Institutes of Health's Response to AIDS."
26. Quoted in Sarah Nelson, "Biologist Flossie Wong-Staal Remembered for Pioneering HIV Research and Treatments," *Daily Bruin*, August 6, 2020. https://dailybruin.com.
27. Quoted in Amanda Heidt, "Pioneering Molecular Virologist Flossie Wong-Staal Dies," *The Scientist*, July 14, 2020. www.the-scientist.com.

Chapter Three: Jenny Han, Author

28. Quoted in Paula Peters Chambers, "Young at Heart," *En Forme*, November 30, 2021. https://enformeva.com.
29. Quoted in Mary Cadden, "*To All the Boys I've Loved Before* Author Jenny Han's Favorite Book as a Young Adult Will Surprise You," *USA Today*, July 17, 2021. www.usatoday.com.
30. Quoted in Cadden, "*To All the Boys I've Loved Before* Author Jenny Han's Favorite Book as a Young Adult Will Surprise You."
31. Quoted in Cadden, "*To All the Boys I've Loved Before* Author Jenny Han's Favorite Book as a Young Adult Will Surprise You."
32. Quoted in Annabel Gutterman, "To All the Boys: *P.S. I Still Love You* Author Jenny Han Gives Her Best Love Advice," *Time*, January 30, 2020. https://time.com.
33. Quoted in Cadden, "*To All the Boys I've Loved Before* Author Jenny Han's Favorite Book as a Young Adult Will Surprise You."
34. Quoted in Cadden, "*To All the Boys I've Loved Before* Author Jenny Han's Favorite Book as a Young Adult Will Surprise You."

35. Quoted in Terry Hong, "An Interview with Jenny Han." Bookslut, May 2011. https://web.archive.org/web/20170827131348/http://www.bookslut.com/features/2011_05_017614.php.
36. Quoted in *Justine Magazine*, *Jenny Han on Writing Tips, Romance, Her Sister & More!*, YouTube, April 17, 2016. www.youtube.com/watch?v=c385teLhxiw.
37. Quoted in Kristen Iversen, "Jenny Han on the Importance of Asian-American Representation in YA and Everywhere," *Nylon*, August 17, 2018. www.nylon.com.
38. Quoted in Rachel Seo, "'Anyone Could Be the Girl Next Door': How Jenny Han Defied Hollywood Typecasting to Turn *The Summer I Turned Pretty* into a Smash Hit," *Variety*, July 28, 2023. https://variety.com.
39. Quoted in Melissa Walker, "Author Jenny Han on Her Bestselling Trilogy's New Book *Always and Forever, Lara Jean*," *Teen Vogue*, May 7, 2017. www.teenvogue.com.
40. Quoted in Elena Nicolaou, "My YA Book Completely Changed My Life—and the Entire Publishing Industry," Refinery 29, April 1, 2019. www.refinery29.com.
41. Jenny Han, "Jenny Kissed Me," Jenny Han personal website, 2023. www.jennyhan.com.
42. Quoted in Karen Han, "Jenny Han Says Some Hollywood Execs Tried to Whitewash *To All the Boys I've Loved Before*, Too," *Teen Vogue*, August 18, 2016. www.teenvogue.com.

Chapter Four: Anna Sui, Fashion Designer

43. Quoted in Tim Blanks, *The World of Anna Sui*. New York: Abrams, 2017, p. 8.
44. Quoted in Emily Mercer, "The Originals: How Anna Sui Became the Gen Z Fashion Whisperer," *Women's Wear Daily*, August 15, 2024. https://wwd.com.
45. Quoted in Ligaya Mishan, "Anna Sui," *New York Times*, October 20, 2021. www.nytimes.com.
46. Quoted in Alyssa Lapid, "Anna Sui Knew She'd Be a Designer at Age Four," Bustle, September 8, 2023. www.bustle.com.
47. Quoted in Guy Trebay, "Anna Sui, Fashion's Favorite Daughter, Gets Her Day in the Sun," *New York Times*, October 3, 2019. www.nytimes.com.
48. Quoted in Lapid, "Anna Sui Knew She'd Be a Designer at Age Four."
49. Quoted in Mishan, "Anna Sui."
50. Quoted in Eddie Roche, "Anna Sui Reflects on 33 Years in Fashion—and What's Coming Next!," *Fashion Week Daily*, September 9, 2024. https://fashionweekdaily.com.
51. Quoted in Lapid, "Anna Sui Knew She'd Be a Designer at Age Four."
52. Quoted in Lapid, "Anna Sui Knew She'd Be a Designer at Age Four."

53. Quoted in Blanks, *The World of Anna Sui.*
54. Quoted in Kyle Munzenrieder, "My Life in Parties: Anna Sui's Punk-Adjacent Youth and Enduring Fashion Friendships," *W*, December 4, 2020. www.wmagazine.com.
55. Quoted in Munzenrieder, "My Life in Parties."
56. Quoted in Munzenrieder, "My Life in Parties."
57. Mishan, "Anna Sui."
58. Quoted in Blanks, *The World of Anna Sui*, p. 217.
59. Faran Krentcil, "How Anna Sui Created Some of Music's Most Iconic Looks," Alternative Press, April 13, 2023. www.altpress.com.

Chapter Five: Mindy Kaling, Actor

60. Mindy Kaling, *Is Everyone Hanging Out Without Me? (And Other Concerns)*. New York: Crown, 2011, p. 35.
61. Quoted in IANS, "Growing Up, No One Looked like Me on TV, Says Mindy Kaling," News 18, May 16, 2020. www.news18.com.
62. Quoted in Diksha Basu, "Mindy Kaling on Why She Uses Her Fame and Fortune to Break Barriers for Indians on the Global Stage," *Vogue India*, December 2, 2020. www.vogue.in.
63. Mindy Kaling, "Mindy Kaling: How I Used What Sucked About High School to Come Out on Top," *Seventeen*, August 11, 2015. www.seventeen.com.
64. Kaling, *Is Everyone Hanging Out Without Me?*, p. 33.
65. Kaling, "Mindy Kaling."
66. Kaling, *Is Everyone Hanging Out Without Me?*, p. 72.
67. Kaling, *Is Everyone Hanging Out Without Me?*, p.89.
68. Quoted in Antonia Blyth, "Mindy Kaling on How *Late Night* Was Inspired by Her Own 'Diversity Hire' Experience & the Importance of Holding the Door Open for Others," Deadline, May 18, 2019. https://deadline.com.
69. Quoted in Nicole Gallucci, "Mindy Kaling Talks TV Representation and the 'Diwali' Episode of *The Office*," Mashable, July 1, 2020. https://mashable.com.
70. Quoted in Rebecca Nelson, "Mindy Kaling Didn't Sign Up to Be a Role Model," *Elle*, October 9, 2019. www.elle.com.
71. Quoted in Basu, "Mindy Kaling on Why She Uses Her Fame and Fortune to Break Barriers for Indians on the Global Stage."
72. Quoted in Blyth, "Mindy Kaling on How *Late Night* Was Inspired by Her Own 'Diversity Hire' Experience & the Importance of Holding the Door Open for Others."
73. Quoted in IANS, "Growing Up, No One Looked like Me on TV, Says Mindy Kaling."
74. Quoted in Blyth, "Mindy Kaling on How *Late Night* Was Inspired by Her Own 'Diversity Hire' Experience & the Importance of Holding the Door Open for Others."

FOR FURTHER RESEARCH

Books

Tim Blanks, *The World of Anna Sui*. New York: Abrams, 2017.

Karen Wang Diggs, *The Book of Awesome Asian Women: Empresses, Warriors, Scientists, and Mavericks*. Miami, FL: Mango, 2025.

Mindy Kaling, *Is Everyone Hanging Out Without Me? (And Other Concerns)*. New York: Crown, 2011.

Judy Tzu-Chun Wu and Gwendolyn Mink, *Fierce and Fearless: Patsy Takemoto Mink, First Woman of Color in Congress*. New York: NYU Press, 2023.

Internet Sources

Bill Branson, “Flossie Wong-Staal, Who Unlocked Mystery of H.I.V., Dies at 73,” *New York Times*, July 17, 2020. www.nytimes.com.

Hadley Freeman, “Mindy Kaling: ‘I Was So Embarrassed About Being a Diversity Hire,’” *The Guardian* (Manchester, UK), May 31, 2019. www.theguardian.com.

Richard Mertens, “Political Pioneer: Patsy Mink, JD’51, Was a Tenacious and Determined Politician,” *University of Chicago Magazine*, September/October 2012. https://mag.uchicago.edu.

Rachel Seo, “‘Anyone Could Be the Girl Next Door’: How Jenny Han Defied Hollywood Typecasting to Turn *The Summer I Turned Pretty* into a Smash Hit,” *Variety*, July 28. 2023. https://variety.com.

Guy Trebay, “Anna Sui, Fashion’s Favorite Daughter, Gets Her Day in the Sun,” *New York Times*, October 3, 2019. www.nytimes.com.

Websites

Asian American Women’s Political Initiative (AAWPI)

www.aawpi.org

The AAWPI is the only political leadership organization in the United States for Asian and Pacific Islander (AAPI) American women. Its website provides information about fellowships the initiative offers for projects that impact the AAPI population and news featuring influential AAPI women.

Asian American Writers' Workshop

https://aaww.org

The Asian American Writers' Workshop supports Asian American writers through workshops, events, open mics, and opportunities for financial support through fellowships. Its website also features the writing of Asian American writers, from poets to journalists and fiction writers.

Center for Asian Pacific American Women

https://capaw.org

This organization helps Asian and Pacific American women build leadership skills and find a supportive network through conferences, fellowships, peer mentoring, and more. A digital library features Asian and Pacific Islander women in different fields making an impact in their communities.

Patsy Mink Foundation

www.patsyminkfoundation.org

Founded in 2003 in Patsy Mink's honor, this foundation continues her legacy of focusing on the needs of children and women. The foundation offers college scholarships to low-income mothers.

Smithsonian American Women's History Museum

https://womenshistory.si.edu

The museum's goal is to expand the story of America through often-untold accounts and accomplishments of women. Pages for middle school and high school students present the stories of women in various fields and from all different backgrounds.

INDEX

Note: Boldface page numbers indicate illustrations.

PICTURE CREDITS

Cover: DFree/Shutterstock

6: The NASA Library/Alamy Stock Photo
10: IanDagnall Computing/Alamy Stock Photo
14: Gado Images/Alamy Stock Photo
16: Associated Press
19: PBH Images/Alamy Stock Photo
22: Science History Images/Alamy Stock Photo
25: Associated Press
29: Gillian Pullinger/Alamy Stock Photo
33: AFF/Alamy Stock Photo
35: Newscom
38: WENN Rights Ltd/Alamy Stock Photo
43: Associated press
45: dpa picture alliance/Alamy Stock Photo
47: BEND IT FILMS/FILM COUNCIL/ROC MEDIA/HELKON MEDIA AG/Album/Newscom
51: PictureLux/The Hollywood Archive/Alamy Stock Photo
53: Scott Kirkland/Sipa USA/Newscom

ABOUT THE AUTHOR

Sara Rowe Mount writes articles and books for children and teens. She has a particular interest in reading about and researching the history of individuals from marginalized populations. She lives in the Northeast with her husband, their daughter, and lots of books.